DATE			

LEARN THE VALUE OF

Honesty

by ELAINE P. GOLEY
Illustrated by Debbie Crocker

ROURKE ENTERPRISES, INC.
VERO BEACH, FL 32964

Library of Congress Cataloging-in-Publication Data

Goley, Elaine P., 1949–
Learn the value of honesty.

Summary: Presents situations that demonstrate the meaning and importance of honesty.
1. Honesty—Juvenile literature. [1. Honesty.
2. Conduct of life] I. Title. II. Title: Honesty.
BJ1533.H7G65 1987 179′.9 87-16289
ISBN 0-86592-385-X

Honesty

Do you know what **honesty** is?

Telling Mom you gave your peas to the dog
is **honesty.**

Honesty is telling your friend that you don't want to play hide and seek.

Paying for your chewing gum before you leave the store is **honesty.**

Honesty is returning your friend's favorite bracelet when you find it.

Playing fair with your friends is being **honest.**

When you tell the cashier at the store that she gave you too much change, you're being **honest.**

Honesty is telling your teacher that you wrote on the blackboard during recess.

Giving your friend his share of the marbles you bought together is being **honest.**

When you tell your dad you made your little brother cry, you're being **honest.**

Honesty is telling your teacher that you didn't do your homework.

If you tell Mom you spent your lunch money on candy, you're being **honest.**

Honesty is telling your piano teacher that you didn't practice your lessons.

When your friend dares you to steal a comic book from the store but you say "no", you're being **honest.**

Telling your mom that you didn't brush your teeth after supper is being **honest.**

Honesty is telling your dad you let the kitten into your bedroom.

When you give back a toy you borrowed from your friend, that's being **honest.**

Honesty is telling the truth and doing what's fair.

Honesty

"Rest time," said Mrs. Pine. "Put your heads on your desks. Close your eyes."

Mrs. Pine stepped into the hall. She spoke with Mr. Snow. They talked about taking the class to the city zoo.

Sue heard a noise. She opened her eyes.

"What's that?" she said to herself.

Sue looked around. Scott was at the back of the room. He was stuffing cookies into his mouth. Scott put a lunch box back onto the shelf and tiptoed to his seat. Sue rested her head on the desk again.

Mrs. Pine came back into the room.

"All right, class, you may get your snacks now," she said.

The children got their lunch boxes.

"Where are my cookies?" cried Tom.

What do you think Sue did?
What would you have done if you were Sue?

Honesty

"I got a new bat and ball," said Gary. "Do you want to play baseball?"

"OK," said José. "Let's play in your yard."

First Gary hit the ball. Up, up into the air it went.

"Nice hit," said José. "Let me try."

Whack! The ball sailed over the fence. It flew closer and closer to Mr. Parks' house. Crash! The boys saw the bedroom window break into pieces.

"Run!" cried José. "Mr. Parks won't catch us." José turned to run.

"No, I'm going to speak to Mr. Parks," said Gary. "Are you coming with me or not?"

Which boy was being **honest?**
What would you have done if you were José?